UNDER HELICON
Journeys in the Mediterranean

Also by the Same Author:

BELOW THE TIDE
War and Peace in Cyprus

UNDER HELICON

Journeys in the Mediterranean

by

PENELOPE TREMAYNE

with illustrations by

GUY GRAVETT

TABB HOUSE

First published 1987
Tabb House, 11 Church Street, Padstow, Cornwall

'The Traveller' was first published by the *Atlantic Monthly* magazine.

The illustrations are by Guy Gravett, except those on pp 48 and 84 belonging to or by the author, that on p. 60 kindly given by Mr John Bertin, and that on p.66 taken by the late Mr Tombazis, the distinguished Athenian photographer, and which his son, Mr A. N. Tombazis, has kindly allowed us to use. Copyrights of these photographs belong to the people named here.

The front cover shows a quayside at Heraklion with, super-imposed on it, a Minoan figured vase from the National Museum, Crete.

British Library Cataloguing in Publication Data
Tremayne, Penelope
   Under Helicon : journeys in the Mediterranean
   I. Title
   828'.91409   PR6070.R36/

ISBN 0 907018 54 8

Text printed and bound in Great Britain by Robert Hartnoll (1985) Ltd.
Dust Jacket and Colour Section printed by Quintrell & Company Limited, Wadebridge, Cornwall.
Typeset by Quintrell & Company Limited, Wadebridge, Cornwall.

Foreword

Of the many books which it has fallen to me to introduce to the public this is the most original and the most distinguished.

The public knows Penelope Tremayne for the bravery with which she endured imprisonment, and the threat to her life, in what we used to call Ceylon. Before that she had an heroic record as a Red Cross field worker in Cyprus, in the dangers of civil war and murderous feuds, when she would not leave her post. She wrote of her experiences in one of the best books ever written about Cyprus.

Her remarkable personality shines through in this new book — the courage in such a phrase as 'death is no subject for fear'.

The book expresses her life-long love of the secret places of the Mediterranean, particularly of Greece — not the beaten track of tourists but the almost trackless wilds of mountains, cliffs, and sea. Haunted places with their myths going back to the dawn of European civilization and their memories of the late war and events in which she bore a part.

The book offers us a diptych of prose and poetry, complemented by Mr Gravett's haunting photographs. Penelope Tremayne is a true, rare poet in this time of the decline of real poetry; the prose is that of a poet, of an accomplishment which I not only admire but envy.

Altogether, it makes a beautiful, a magical book, — the expression of a strange spirit — one worthy to become a classic.

A. L. Rowse

PARTANT POUR PARTIR

Mais les vrais voyageurs sont ceux-là seuls qui partent
Pour partir: coeurs légers . . .
Baudelaire.

Partant dès le jour, ainsi
que les phoques, aux coeurs légers,
on a fait escale ici
à Corfou, ensorcelé.

Telles escales, à n'importe où
— Phéacie, les côtes d'Ophir —
nous enivrent, et font de nous
victimes d'un divin délire.

Ferme les yeux, et scelle ton coeur
contre Phéacie, Ophir,
si — insensé voyageur —
tu veux jamais revenir.

Contents

SOMMIÈRES

Why, can we not go southward
and live beneath the vine
on brandy and on barley-bread
and peaches and red wine?

— What should we do for owls at dusk,
and cliffs, and clotted cream,
and coverlets of silken rain
on hills of mist and dream?

Why, lose the leaves and half-lights
and live beneath the vine
on rocks and resin and the sun,
and octopus and wine.

— What should we do for coral trees
a mile below the blue,
and basking turtles, and the breeze
that blows from Xingalu?

Why, leave the leaning palm trunks
and live beneath the vine,
on scent of fig-trees in the sun,
and starlight in the wine.

ROMANCE

Now we'll set course into the morning sun
with tall sails spearing up against the gold,
sharp-edged and shadowed like the blue-grey wings
of gulls that tip and veer upon the wind.

And just as gulls that slice the morning light
hover and lift, and tilt, and plunge away
down the abysses of the trackless air,
so shall we at the wind's touch ride the water,
and strew in white behind the sickle prow
the cut sheaves of the tender, flax-flower sea.

Where are your dusky orange groves? What worth
your barren heights and burning desert shores?
What worth your blue and dim Sicilian hills
all veiled in ancient splendour? For we sail
to find the star-sown islands of our dreams,
where dolphins linger for Dionysus
and winds bear names; and through the fire of noon
the soft sea, sleeping, curls against the shore.

But if you ask, are there such isles as these?
Look in your heart, and see them mirrored there.

ROMANCE

The most honoured of the winds is Aeolus, who is not
limited to a compass point of his own, and is credited
with having fathered both the Achaean and the Dorian
races. He ruled so wisely and well that when Death
reached him Zeus removed him to the Lipari Islands in
the Tyrrhenian Sea and there gave him command of all
the winds, to let in and out of their caves as he thought
fit. His sons, descendants of the grey-eyed goddess
Athene, carried the Greek blood far through the
Mediterranean.

Boreas, the north wind, was said to be the oldest of the
winds themselves. His name means the Devourer, but in
very early myths he was the creator of all things,
fertilising Eurynome, the first goddess to rise out of
Chaos, as she danced southwards to keep herself warm
from his cold blast. He was later (and in fact up to the
seventeenth century, because of Pliny's weighty
authority) thought to be able to impregnate mares in the
same way. The spring was held to be of his begetting,
born after the bitter winter gestation; and anyone can see
the logic of this idea who knows the freakish force of the
Meltemi, the northerly wind that blows down the
Aegean in the parched Greek summer.

The link between Dionysus and the dolphin is difficult
to disentangle, but very old. Many of the tales tell that
the god was mishandled by pirates, and turned them all
into dolphins; but that would hardly reflect them as the
companions and allies that they seem always to have
been. Perhaps they befriended him during the time
when he hid in Thetis' cave under the sea; or more likely
the connexion is through Arion, a worshipper of
Dionysus or perhaps an aspect of him. Arion was

thrown overboard by a false friend who envied him his musical skill, but was rescued and brought to shore by dolphins. I cannot help thinking that the two stories are really the same, and that the pirates were brought into it by later sceptics, unready to believe in anything good under the sun.

OVER SANTORIN

Sky and sea, and sea and sky
each to each is upside-down.
In the solid, perfect blue
countless clouds and islets lie
broadcast, by the sea-wind through
stainless air and water sown.

Clouds like cliffs of sunlit ice
crowned with foam rise sheer and clear;
peach-red archipelago,
shadowed gorge and precipice,
far above and far below
piled and roseate, appear.

And the eyes that look on these
to the heart their message bear:
joy and grief together lie,
foam-engendered mysteries
mirrored, like the sea and sky:
one substantial, one of air.

UNDER HELICON

Softly, on the secret shore
shifting ripples lift and sleep,
lapse and fall; and, cool and deep,
fill the bay; and say no more.

White and pink the speaking stones,
ground and smooth and round and bright,
lend an echo, crisp and light,
to the water's living tones.

Silent, on the secret strand
shed the blackness; shed the dreams.
Slough the cruel, false extremes
swiftly, on the vivid sand.

Pain impedes us; say no more.
Masks are liars. Lay your own
with the silvered rocks, alone,
soundless, on the secret shore.

UNDER HELICON

I had been walking for three days, mostly without paths, by sun and stars and a rough sense of direction; with a lump of dried bread, two tomatoes, and the sea to drink, washed down with occasional mouthfuls from a pint flask of hoarded fresh water.

The tilted little shore, perhaps thirty yards across, lay at the base of a two-hundred-foot silver-grey cliff from which one or two stunted cypress trunks leaned yearningly out and down. The beach was made entirely of pink and white pebbles and shells. At the far side they were ground to rough sand, and had a slightly darker colour than the shell-pink of the rest; and here the cliffs, stepping forward to form as it were a cove within a cove, were so tall and overhanging that even now, near mid-day, a strip of shade slept at their feet. The water, of an intense blue-green tranquillity, just stirred along its edge the pink and white stones, which whispered back with a sound like the faintest and most distant of sheep-bells. The place was virgin.

Knees shaking from the climb down the cliff, I stripped and plunged into the sea. Cool and quiet and dark beneath the dazzle, it was blessed as only the elements themselves can be, filling and flooding the senses, lapping the limbs and slipping through the dusty disquiet of the mind. I drank, and dived, and drank, and drifted; and, lying alternately above the water's edge and below it, washed away the burning climax of the morning.

Later I heard that, though fishing boats very occasionally passed, they never put in here, for the bay was sacred (to whom, it was not clear); and the deity who owned it drowned anyone who entered it. Had I not noticed its extraordinary colour? they added, to bring the subject into the present day. It was because the bay is bottomless, and the current sucks down swimmer or boat.

It is not easy to express the passion for solitude that had possessed me during the preceding days. The emptier grew the mountains round me, the more perfectly did my mood give to them; and I was glad to live on bread and sea-water, and so be able to keep to the empty, unpastured mountains and the totally desolate, because waterless, shores. It was a world made up of stone and salt water and sunlight; and it seemed right that, for a time, one's needs should be cut down to what these could supply. (I quickly and painfully learned, though, that they cannot support one for very long.)

Another need had gone unfulfilled for a long time: the need to find something that could never be made plain with the help of food and drink and comfort, or any kind of company. By the time I reached the secret shore I was exhausted enough to be able at last to look down not only into the quivering, tantalising blue-green of self-regard but also into the clear blackness of facts: of the irrelevance of pain and illusion to the real substance of life. The water to my parched weariness promised a luxurious fulfillment of physical needs; then lapped my limbs again and again in a coolness laden with salt denial. But also it was like looking into a well: the water far down and obscured, but glimmering rationally to the light above: black, and blood-hot, but fit for restoring life.

Berengaria's Window

FOURTOUNA IN AUGUST

The photograph on the opposite page is taken through a stone window-frame in the castle of St Hilarion, and shows how the mountains drop sheer to the coast on which Fourtouna stands, two or three thousand feet below. Richard Coeur de Lion came to Cyprus on his way to the Crusades, and his mother and sister brought to him Berengaria, the daughter of Sancho the Wise of Navarre, to marry. Richard's fleet was driven on shore by an April storm and the deplorable pseudo-Emperor Isaac Comnenus, to whom no harm had been done or intended, attacked it and plundered the wrecks. But treachery is not always profitable: it cost him his island, and Coeur de Lion put him in chains made of silver (since he begged not to be fettered with common iron), and married Berengaria and took her to St Hilarion to look down from that great stone window on her bridegroom's new conquest. I cannot help thinking that even then the island must have been wrapped in its strange, glittering atmosphere of broken promises, broken hopes, and burgeoning illusions.

Fourtouna, a name for the west wind, was a house on a little promontory with its own otherwise inaccessible beach. It had cool stone floors and great equilateral arches, and most happily combined the Spartan with the luxurious. Just inside the gate was a tiny chapel dedicated to St George.

I was new to Cyprus when my friend Marie was building Fourtouna, and I had no inkling of how things would go in the island: of the scale and inevitability of the catastrophe that lay ahead. But exaltation carries its own kind of insight. That night in August I sensed something of the debacle to come. The poem 'Mesaoria

1974' was written after it.

Destruction overtook Marie, too, elsewhere. There are certain people — and in my experience they have always been the most delightful and best — on whose shoulders the claws of the Furies seem almost visibly set.

FOURTOUNA IN AUGUST

The headlong night was all our own;
the ripened moon, the wine, the sea,
the pulsing, willow-pussy stars,
the peacocks and the poetry.

Like tides the glasses rose and fell;
we loved and fought outrageously
and, drunk on words as much as wine,
swam naked in the moon-washed sea.

The hills were dark, and to the shore
an island air came faint and free.
The world was breaking: this we knew,
but would not mourn it formally.

ELONAS

The Monastery of Elonas stands above Leonidhion in Cynuria, on the way from the East Coast to Sparta. The first time I went there, in 1955, it was not reachable by road at all. My two companions and I crossed by fishing-boat from Nauplia to Astros and then walked southwards, our shadows growing alongside us as we went, through vines and cucumber fields, then olive groves, and at last thyme and myrtle and the dark, prickly-leaved scrub oak called *pounari* that clothes the mountain sides as roughly as a hair-shirt. We had been told that presently the track would die and we should have to find our own way on, but we were not prepared for the suddenness with which it died. The sun had broken into long splinters of glory and gone down behind the Parnon range, dusk had given way to a warm, feathery darkness full of little owls, and still the stones had been levelled by other feet. And then, quite suddenly, a hewn cliff stood before us like a wall, straight across the path and plunging on down the last fifty feet or so to the sea. It was like the Pied Piper's passage into the mountain.

The moon was not yet up. By the faint light of surf and stars glimmering along the shore-line we stumbled to and fro, trying to find a way over the shoulder of the cliff or else along the sea-edge at its feet. At last we began to climb straight up the side of the mountain, away from the sea; and after an hour or more, very out of breath and burning with scratches, we reached the crest of the ridge. The moon was near rising now, and we plodded and stumbled on in the thinning darkness until she was well up. Then by her light we chose a place less stony and thorny than the rest, and between the boulders lay down to sleep.

Sunrise woke us, and revealed the solitary splendour of our night's lodging. We had slept in a palace, walled with blue air, scented and rustling, cascading with staircases of wind-polished white stone, carpeted with dark, aromatic green, and roofed with golden light. For mile upon blue mile our mountain kingdom rolled away, and never a road or a house or a cheese-maker's hut to spoil the solitude. We followed the curve of the hill downwards; presently the ground dropped away steeply to a cliff at the foot of which glittered a little rocky bay. Beyond it the sea, drawing the light into itself like a crystal, burned from one headland to the next; and into this dazzle moved slowly, black against the brilliance, a small boat rowed by two men.

We shouted; and the off-shore dawn wind carrying our voices to them they looked up, then backed their oars and put in towards the shore. It must have taken us half an hour to get down; but when at last we came out onto the little strand, there they were, the boat riding gently in a foot of water and their faces full of well-held curiosity.

The Greek countryman is never importunate. His manners are a matter of tradition and deviate scarcely at all from those described in the Odyssey — except, happily, that the exchanges of bronze tripods that went on so freely then no longer take place. I have often wondered about those tripods. Well stocked with them as the average palace must have been, perhaps they were simply what the early upper-class swagman boiled his billy on.

In some districts, when two strangers meet, the rider must first greet a walker, the walker a sitter. This is an imported custom, from the Arabs by way of the Turks. But in other regions it is often the other way round, and the resident must first greet the incomer — as when Edwardian ladies called on one another. I do not know what was politely done in Byzantium.

In either case the initial questions that follow are formal: Where from? Whither going? Thereafter, unless the traveller has revealed himself to be an enemy or a boor, a kind of treaty exists, and the way is open for hospitality, comradeship, or whatever the circumstances may allow.

When the boatmen learned that we were going to Leonidhion they offered to take us aboard. On foot, they said, we should need a day and a half, two days perhaps. The path, once found, wandered to and fro provokingly in the hills. But they would take us by boat to Tiro, where no doubt we could join Andreas, who would be going down in his boat to-day to Sabateki. *Me to Theo*, with God, we should make Leonidhion well before nightfall.

The sea washing our dusty feet deliciously as we clambered inboard, we set off with them. They seemed very lightly loaded: we learned before we left them that they were smugglers, with a consignment, I think (naturally we did not ask them), of cigarette papers. There was a heavy tax on these at the time, whereas tobacco, being home-grown, was cheap. They were hard-working, devout and merry, and did not let their trade interfere with their natural hospitality towards strangers. Nor did they seek to involve us in it, beyond asking us to sit tight and keep our feet on certain boxes at their first stopping-place. There were five houses here, and a man with a peaked cap and a very untrusting eye, who walked out to the end of the ricketty jetty where we tied up. But when he heard from the boatmen that we were strangers and guests he said no more, though he watched suspiciously while two innocent-looking sacks were handed ashore.

On the next lap towards Tiro we crossed a tiny bay with a beach of smooth grey shingle. So calm was the water here that each wave fell and drew back in just the same place as its predecessor, and the shingle was sculpted into broad scallops as regular as those of a giant shell. Here surely, not in the treacherous cross-currents of Paphos, Aphrodite ought to have come ashore.

At Tiro we found Andreas, who loaded us along with his guiltless cargo of bread and melons for Sabateki; and thence, I cannot in the least remember how (except that the last lap was by boat) we reached Leonidhion in the late afternoon.

The harbour lies midway along a deep, curved shingle beach, silvered and fluffy with oleander. There were a few houses near the quayside, and a taverna built of straw mats. A long, thick stone mole ran far out across the bay, giving some easterly shelter to a dangerously open anchorage. A few miles above and behind the harbour lay a small village, planted across a ridge running up into the mountains rather as if it were the saddle on a mule's back. Similar spurs rise one behind another in ascending line, each capped at its tip by a windmill. At their backs, tremendous red-brown cliffs soar upwards to the shoulders of Parnon, completely shutting in the harbour, the village, and a tiny, fertile valley. Into this the river Daphnon has cut itself a little, bouldery gorge filled with noise and spray, falling steeply from the rain-fed summits.

An ancient Doric dialect was still in use here, especially among the women, who were unschooled. They called this language Tsakonika; which had once been Lakonika, they said, but time had eaten the L and given them Ts instead. At the taverna they loaded us with food and drink and welcome; and all three went rather to our heads, for it was a good many hours since we had eaten. We were urged to stay: overnight, to rest ourselves, or until next week, when there was to be a wedding; or for ever, like castaways on the shores of the Land of the Lotus-eaters. But somehow it remained fixed in our own minds that we were on our way to Sparta, and on our way to it that very night, meaning to use the cool of the evening and the light of the moon to cover as much ground as we could.

It is hard now to see why exactly we left this private Paradise so precipitately. Probably we had a limited total time, and in the manner of beginners wanted to travel as far as possible in distance, as much as in depth or experience. In the course of journeys more pleasure and more knowledge are missed through the urge to hurry onwards than in any other way.

When at last we had convinced our hosts that we must go, they got out for us their greatest treasure. It was a 'bus: very ancient and curious-looking but in working order, and it plied, now and then when it was needed, over the three miles or so of good white dust road that ran between the village and the quay. It had been brought over piecemeal in a caique from the Piraeus, and assembled on the jetty; and since there was no road out of the gorge through the great ring of the mountains it was marooned here for ever, barring miracles or a road being built.

When it had taken us to the limit of its domain there were long and warm and vinous farewells. The driver said that it was many, many hours' walking to Kosmas, the next village, for it lay across the watershed from here, looking down upon the plain of Sparta. But there was one port of call on the way, he said. It was a great and famous monastery, though the track to it was so small that we might easily miss it in the dark. There we should find a welcome, and beds for what might remain of the night.

We had no great wish for this. Probably we were still a little drunk on the thyme and starlight of the night before, as well as the last few hours' hospitality. The villagers took us across a high-arched mule bridge and set us on a little track that followed the river, climbing and winding away up into the last of the daylight, with the heat still hammering off the rocks. As we trudged, we watched the sunset burn out against a towering wall of interlocking cliffs as dark as blood. Below us the bottom of the gorge was now dry and grey-white, like old bones. Darkness came down and still we were twisting upwards; only a rare goat-bell and the sounds of our own clumsier movements reminded us that we were still in an inhabited world. Doubt began to arise in our minds about whether there really was any monastery at all. It had not seemed to matter, earlier; but now, for the sake of keeping the real world in line with the legendary one, we wanted it to be there. We had failed to take in, or had simply not been told, how far away it was; a matter of twenty-five kilometres as it turned out, and growing steeper all the way.

Presently a late moon ringed the stones in our path with sharp black shadows. We went on winding in and out of the rocks, and this stony, moonlit world seemed to have no mortal end. Then, as we rounded yet another cliff shoulder, we saw it: eight hundred feet above us — and nearly vertically above us at that — plastered against the rock under the brow of a cliff like a swallow's nest or those Tibetan lamaseries of which one sees tantalising photographs taken by tougher, luckier travellers than oneself. The whole structure was inexplicably hung with lights from end to end, and glittered above our astonishment like the lamps of Heaven. It was hard for a moment to believe that it was not all an hallucination. But the lime-whitened walls dwindling down into the rock, the buttresses and cramps and tiers of lighted balconies, were all solid enough; and after another half-hour's climbing and two false casts, there before us was the path, in places more like a ladder, that led zig-zag up the cliff like the path to Paradise. Long before we reached them the lights had bewilderingly all gone out. But after a while we heard voices shouting down directions to us. Angles of masonry gleamed, first above, then away to one side, and at last below us; for since monasteries of this kind are built on props out of the surface of the rock, the only way into them is from above.

At last we reached a low hut against a piece of wall along a ledge at the gate. A young man stumbled up from where he had been sleeping and led us down a steeply-tilted, tunnel-like path built tight-in to the cliff. At the end of it was a narrow, arched gateway, and a bell handle. The young man seized this and pulled with all his might: an immense length of wire uncoiled in his hands but he went on reeving it in and presently, far away, a half-hearted jangle started. Lights appeared again, the wooden door creaked open, and we were led inside and made welcome.

It was during the fifteen-day fast before the Feast of the Assumption of the Blessed Virgin: the monks apologised because they could offer us no better food than black bread, olives, and tomatoes. But these tasted like manna to us, and the pitchers of vintage rain-water that they carried up seemed better than the best champagne. A little, slender old monk, half mad and half saint, entertained us gravely while we ate, with childlike prattle intersown with accounts of miracles which, for him personally or within his knowledge, the

Blessed Virgin had performed here. He had been the subject of a miraculous cure, about which he was not in the least boastful — as people are who have been, say, to a fashionable bone-setter. He had been taken mysteriously ill: he could neither eat nor drink nor move, and bit by bit he grew blind. This continued for three months, and he was given up for lost. But the Blessed Virgin, to whom he and the others had prayed, cured him in three days; and since then he had not ceased to glorify her name.

Brother Gerasimo (I still have a letter from him) is dead now. The track we followed has vanished, and a tarmac road extends to the gate itself, where a great car-park blasted out of the side of the mountain awaits pious travellers by the 'bus-load. But the Leonidhion 'bus will not be among them. By now it too must have died: perhaps of a broken heart. The brethren sell tinfoil charms in the forecourt. Cigarette packets and orange-peel proliferate, and the mountain stillness is loud with revving engines and the animating cries of hot cross babies.

ELONAS

Now we'll take the holy road
(the stones clink hymns beneath our hooves):
leave the wine-loud village street,
leave the well-head cool and sweet,
worn by the rope to twenty grooves.
[1] *"Ελα, αλογάκι μου.*

High against the appearing stars
that watch us, smiling silently,
hangs the abode of holy peace,
white as freedom, blue as Greece,
bound with the cords of sanctity.
[2] *"Ωπα! χελιδόνι μου.*

Steep as death our pathway now
and narrow as eternity.
Faint our laughter falls away
down the valley, down the day,
lost in the rocks — and so are we.
[3] *Νά τό δρόμο· μπράβο σου.*

Turn the cliff, and turn again:
the gate of grace stands tall and true.
Hard the road from here to there:
make your cross and lift a prayer.
God and the wine will bring us through.
[4] *Φθάσαμε πουλάκι μου.*

Now the silence; now the peace.
In holy calm our souls shall grow.
Here we'll live, on bread and wine,
peace of Christ and candle-shine
— now, till the dawn: an age to go.
[5] *Παψε περιστέρι μου.*

Footnotes: 1 Come, on, my little horse. 2 Hold up, my swallow. 3 There's
the path. Well done! 4 We've got there, my little bird. 5 Hush, my dove.

CITHAERON

You cannot bend the level light nor hold the gold of morning
        trembling on the azimuth of day.
The world will turn, for all you will, and mid-day dim the dawning,
        burning on the water of the bay.

The spring that brings the turtle-doves and sets the swallows wheeling
        plays along the water like a flame;
the summer comes, the sacred fire, the molten hills revealing
        stripped of all the veils of love and shame.

The lives of men are brief and frail and full of fleeting glories:
        thirst for love and knowledge, strength and art;
the flame will sear away the false and leave unscathed the flawless,
        burning as the spirit burns the heart.

Oh never mock the turtle-dove across the myrtle calling,
        calling in the morning of desire;
yet fair as falls the slanted light, and soft the feathers falling,
        Phoenix never rose but from the fire.

CITHAERON

Fishermen on the coast had warned me that I could not cross the promontory under which their two or three houses sheltered. Even men hardly ever did so, and then only in winter (it was August now), and several together, so as to carry enough drinking-water between them, for it took about three days. But I knew — or thought I knew — that one does not die of thirst in that time, even in great deserts. So I had thanked my advisers and gone on my way.

It was hard to imagine that anything could match the beauty and the gaunt, merciless loneliness of these hills, steeped as they are in myth and history and refracting an almost tactile sense of the joy and laughter and unheeding savagery of nature itself: truth without the veil of pity. It seemed to shimmer off the rock with the same intensity as the sunlight, as dry as the ringing limestone, as vibrant as the air. The distance between death and the pinnacle of life could be seen to be infinitesimal, the difference between them gigantic, and the chance that allots them as irrevocable and trivial as the lightest flurry of air.

It is said that Dionysus was born on Cithaeron. Certainly it was the home of his worshippers, the Maenad maidens, and of their fearful revels in his honour, which began by celebrating the clear, brilliant onrush of physical joy, and swept up to an ecstatic triumph in which the Maenads ran wild over the mountain and tore into bloody shreds any live thing, human or animal, that they came upon.

Cithaeron was thickly forested then; and even now a few of its slopes are dark with pines. But the greater part of it is a wilderness of tough, thorny cover, sheer, sometimes huge, precipices, and stretches of bare, glittering rock. There is no water at all on the mountain now. Winter brings up a few trickles, and then the shepherds move down from the high pastures where there are springs; but for at least two months, at the time when I was there, these lower slopes had been empty of men and flocks.

Threading painfully among the thorns and stones, about mid-day, I came suddenly upon the torn-off hind leg of an animal, lying on the ground. It was from no possible fox or sheep-dog. Size and paw and claws and hair all spoke of wolf: improbable, but not totally inconceivable, for if the shepherds of Parnassus, to the southward, are to be believed, a rare wolf is still sometimes glimpsed there. But what could have happened here? The thing had not yet begun to decay, nor much to dessicate. The bone had been broken clean through, like a stick, just below the stifle-joint, and the flesh and fur had shrunk back, so that nearly an inch of dead-white bone was exposed. There was nothing to suggest what kind of blow or wound had been given, from what direction; and there were no other lacerations, or even marks, on the leg or the paw.

I stood for a long time in that blazing emptiness of sun, wondering. A trap? But if a wild animal had so desperately torn itself free, the trap would still have been there; and it was not. I searched a wide space for it. An eagle, perhaps, then? Could some great bird of prey have found a dead, dismembered wolf or jackal, or fought and killed one; carried off a limb, and dropped it here, out of sight of the battle-ground? This side of fairy-tale, it seemed unlikely. Then what? Could there be still, among the herdsmen of Cithaeron, a lingering trace of the cult of Dionysus that, once in a long while, perhaps, broke to the surface with some grisly ritual in which a living animal was once more torn limb from limb? I could not believe it.

None the less, Cithaeron is a curious mountain; very empty, full of light and an impression of laughter and hot cruelty, of great beauty and unaccountable quiet. On other mountains one may feel as much at home as the foxes or the roots of the trees. On Cithaeron one is, not exactly a stranger, but an ant that has strayed out of line. Instinct is to stay very quiet and keep one's eyes very wide open, and learn as much as possible of the place before one is caught out.

But caught by what? Perhaps only by ignorance, which may catch one out anywhere; perhaps by the peculiarly foolish form of ignorance which is fear.

MESAORIA 1974

Stavrovouni like a star
hangs above the blood-soaked plain.
Never in faith your feet shall find
the path to climb those heights again,
    out of the labyrinth heart of the hills,
      the laughing and desolate depths of the hills.

Innocence and grace were yours,
tokens of eternal youth
warm as the spring; but not the heart
to love your friend, or search for truth
    over the languorous, luminous hills,
      the maculate, delicate, leopard-marked hills.

Stavrovouni hollow stands
stooped upon the holy Wood.
Blacker than hell the ambient air,
it smells of fear, and tastes of blood,
    staining the sun as it falls on the hills,
      the cruel and jewelled and flower-strewn hills.

Icarus the falling-star
flaming, sets alight the skies.
None that has known you but shall grieve
for your rejected paradise
    flung to the dogs on the flanks of the hills,
      the tawny and tender and heart-breaking hills.

Stavrovouni

MESAORIA 1974

The monastery of Stavrovouni stands on the summit of a pinnacle-like hill, the product of wind-erosion, looking out over the Mesaoria, the central plain of Cyprus. It commands particular reverence among the Cypriots because of its two greatest treasures: a fragment of the True Cross and a portrait on wood said to have been painted by St Luke himself. But in spite of the holiness that these relics ought surely to inspire, the monks were led astray by the lure of politics in the 1950s, and gave shelter and aid to known murderers and a fair wind to terrorism. I saw them in the days of their pride, when to go up to the church was to chance being shot on the way by someone whom they were protecting and were continuing to protect; and I saw it again many years later, when the wheel had come full-circle and of the many villages and churches to be seen from the monastery walls there was not one that had not been burned and looted by the Turks, or where the crescent of Islam on its blood-red field was not flowering.

AYIOS THYRSOS

The shore with rocks like roses
and whitened wreaths is strewn,
where the long slow tides come by
like a dying tune.

And the swallows crying in the sea-caves
— crying when the dawn is new —
tell of the griefs of long ago,
unassuaged, untrue;
and how the bright life still runs high
though the heart break in two.

AYIOS THYRSOS

Ayios Thyrsos is a hauntingly attractive place, bare and spray-cooled, all browns and blues and whites; its dark, flat-topped rocks pitted with salt, its tiny bights of sand starred with beach flotsam, and here and there a dark fishing net, hoisted between stakes for mending, aquiver in the light wind.

The swallows nest inside the sea-caves and flash in and out in the clear, early morning sunlight, blue-backed, like souls in and out of the nether world.

Saint Thyrsos was martyred in the year 250 at Caesarea. He had first been beaten with iron bars, and anointed with boiling lead. He had been put in a copper pot to boil, but the pot cracked and the water ran out, and no one seems to have had any heart for a roast. He was thrown to the lions but they refused to eat him. He prayed for, obtained, and survived an earthquake which overthrew the statues of the gods that he had been ordered to honour. Finally he was sewn up in a sheet and sawn by four men who worked at him for many hours unsuccessfully, for the saw-blade kept turning. But after they had exhausted themselves the saint prayed to God, and rendered up his soul at last of his own accord.

It is not at all surprising that this good and durable man should be remembered; and why not at a rock on the northern shore of Cyprus as well as anywhere else? And yet my mind fills with pagan doubts. It seems he had no connection whatever with Cyprus; and there is another figure who had.

The *thyrsos* was the rod tipped with a pine-cone which the Maenads carried as weapons in the routs of Dionysus. In Cypriot mythology Ariadne was not a maiden betrayed, but a birth-goddess, and Dionysus was the father of her many children. She had a temple at

Amathus, a place of much holy resort and renown, where she was worshipped together with Aphrodite. In one legend Dionysus, enraged by her profanation with Theseus of his grotto in Naxos, had her killed in child-bed.

Ariadne as a Cyprian goddess had a feast-day on September 2nd, when a young man climbed down into her tomb and there went through the motions of child-birth; credible-sounding conduct for the self-mutilated transvestite priests of Dionysus. The Dionysiac frenzy culminated in horror; in most of the stories, in the dismembering and cannibalising of children or young men. One tale records that the three daughters of King Minyas, who would not join the revels, were punished first with the Maenad madness and then with death and transformation into swallows.

Perhaps the dedication to Ayios Thyrsos is simply a veil over a name that really recalls rites practised in that place a thousand years before the holy man was sawn in half. And I should like to believe that the voices of the swallows which now echo under one's feet with their mysterious note of lost, desperate imaginary tragedy, have sounded so since the days when men said that the swallows had once been young girls.

Honesty compels me to admit that the destruction of the daughters of King Minyas took place not in Cyprus but on Mount Cithaeron in Boeotia, the reputed birthplace of Dionysus in Greece. He has other reputed birthplaces in other countries, too.

I did not even know the name of the saint when I first went to Ayios Thyrsos, let alone the possibility of the place having any link with the bloody Dionysiac rite. But I did to some extent have in mind, because the swallows' voices irresistibly recalled it, the tale of Itylus and the nightingale.

St Hilarion

SOUND AND EFFECT

There is a spine of mountains nearly three thousand feet high that runs up the northern shore of Cyprus. It is unique, at least in my limited experience, in being only a single mountain thick, like a cardboard stage set, and it twists up the length of the island like the jagged frill of bone along the dorsal ridge of some vast, dead saurian. Four points along it stand out from the main rock-line; St Hilarion, Buffavento, Pentadactylos and Cantara. The names alone are like a cavalcade. The crusaders thought these heights perfect strongholds for siege, sally, and defence, and built castles on them, but without success. St Hilarion, the most famous, did serve its turn, but was not impregnable when it came to the crunch, either in the thirteenth century when Richard Coeur de Lion took it from the emperor Isaac Comnenus, or in our own time, when the Greek-Cypriots took it in the teeth of invasion from the Turkish army. The highest point of the range, Buffavento, might perhaps have been impregnable if it had ever been possessable except by the eagles. The ruins crown it still, of a castle only half built, abandoned because the difficulties of bringing up men, materials, and supplies proved too great. But the real explanation of this failure may lie in the Cypriot character. No one who has seen the monasteries of the Meteora in Thessaly, built in the fourteenth century as strongholds as well as places of holy retreat, can accept that Buffavento was truly too hard to build upon. Man-power could have done the job: after Richard had gone it must have been will-power that was lacking.

Beyond Buffavento is Pentadactylos, the Five Fingers, which remained unburdened with mediæval bastion-work for a better reason: the rock is so rotten and crumbling that it is scarcely to be climbed, let alone built upon. But the stubby grey digits standing up vertically out of a slight depression in the mountain chain look very fierce and imposing, and like enough to a primitive hand to justify the name.

I drove across the Mesaoria one day just after an illness, feeling my Land Rover between my hands again like an old friend, half watching the road and half watching the line of the mountains on my left, through the hours of a bright, stormy March afternoon slanting towards a tumultuous sunset. I had listened through three days to much talk amounting to nothing, and to some fine propositions that could only have come to life had various facts, as bare and intractable as the mountains themselves, been what they were not. The correspondence between words and thunder-clouds was irresistible.

SOUND AND EFFECT

Above long billowy plumy trails
of plum-blue wreathed and rose-wet air
stood Buffavento and the Five
like diorite, unmoved and bare,

while fierce as breakers, cold as knives,
about them beat the bolt-bright veils
that clamourous as a thousand wives
swirled formless at the wind's nine tails.

SARONIKO

Here in this world of blanched and gleaming stone,
of salt and thyme and brilliant air — this white
prismatic world of concentrated light —
all life is ours, and nothing is our own.

And this is god-like, this is to be free,
untouched, in this clear aether born again;
brimming with wonder, and fierce love, and pain,
and laughter, deep and quenchless as the sea.

MOZART AND MPENITSES

This silence, made of olive leaves
and sunlight and the opening rose,
of lizards' footfalls as they climb
and pomegranate blossom, shows
how light, with sound and stillness, weaves
a net of joy, outside of time.

Softness of flute and violin
invades the silence. Loose-cut sheaves
of sunlight and of music fall
between the slanting swallows' wings,
and green vine-fingers on the wall,
probing the rough, warm stones, expose
how life may master man-made things
and sorrows melt when songs begin.

BOCCANEGRA

The road here wound up the hill, and alongside it, to seaward, ran the high, plastered and cream-washed wall of my father's house. It was very long; the first barred and shuttered window was a good fifteen feet from the ground, but because of the gradient each following window was relatively lower, and the last one was less than three feet up. The wall extended beyond the end of the house, and in it was a green-painted wooden door, with a cypress tree beside it and a big iron bell-pull. The cockled red roof-tiles were old and worn with sun and rain, and a little square turret, with four shuttered windows round it and a pointed cap of roof, crowned the house. A monastery, one would have guessed; or just possibly an orphanage or convent-school.

Then you opened the green door. Behind it was a wrought-iron gate; and behind that was what looked like fairy-land. A small square of gravel, decorated with the fluffiest of pepper trees, gave access on one side to the door of the house and at the other to a cascade of terraced garden paths and brilliant falls of hanging flowers. In front, a low wall edged the gravel space, and beyond it was nothing but blue air and the glitter of the sea 600 feet below.

The garden spilled down the cliff to within the last fifty feet or so of the shore, in successive terraces, each narrower and higher than the last, twisting along the contour of the cliff; ablaze with aloes, tufted with the great, silver-blue sabres of the agaves; splashed with black caverns of shade from huge pine trees and flickering groves of olive trees, their trunks twisted and knotted and pocked into rings and whirlpools, as the surface of water is marked by an undercurrent. Dozens of tiny flights of steps, a single stone wide, ran down like rivulets from one terrace to the next; and from the topmost path that ran, arcaded, just below the house, you looked at the sea through the rustling tops of the trees two, or ten, terraces down. Through the surface of this path, too, rose the smooth trunk of a majestic eucalyptus tree; its branches shading the roof of the house and its roots buried twenty feet below, under the arcade.

At dusk the garden was full of the croaking of bull-frogs who lived in the two big cisterns. Straddled on broad water-lily leaves they bellowed at each other through the evening, their throats vibrating like drum-tops; if you came a step nearer they plopped off with a noise like corks out of bottles into the greenish water, leaving a gap of hollow silence in which you suddenly heard the sawing of the cicadas.

During the day, sea and air were one as bright as the other; and at night the lights of the anchovy-fishing boats made the dark sea into a twinkling sky. It was a place for imagination to take wing from.

The house has passed into the hands of strangers now. I wonder how much of its power has taken wing from it, or whether it has been stronger than the Lombard hordes?

Boccanegra

BOCCANEGRA

The night is full of stars and fishing-boats,
and the slim moon on every ripple floats
a gilded fish, all bright
and slippery dipping on the night.

The day is all a running fire of gold
and olive-leaves, and sea-foam silver-cold;
and the bright molten sea
is liquid lapis lazuli.

Here a gilt dawn spills over, flushed and clear,
down the blue, misty mountain walls; and here,
come you by day or night,
shall be a new dawn of delight.

CAVES

These curved, low caves like empty dragons' mouths
pluck at the mind and, in their silent way,
stir images as clear as they are old.
One — or perhaps a hundred — of their like,
dry and sheep-scented, close the labyrinth
that sheltered Zeus a million days ago.
In one the child Christ shivered where he lay,
feeling the rough straw cold.
These are the sacred places, you should know:
the cradle and the fold.

CAVES

The caves closing the Labyrinth are not in this case the Dictaean Caves themselves, those bottomless, dripping, reverberting crypts of mystery and pre-history. I meant those innocent, open-lipped, shallow refuges in the flanks of God knows how many mountains, which shepherds still use and have always used. At one side of such a cave, where the floor curves up towards the low roof, the rock will have been cut, or in soft sandstone scooped away, to make a feed-trough: the Manger of the story, just as the caves are the first true Inns of the world. On the other side of the cave, more cutting may have made a ledge or dais, a few inches higher than the rest of the floor and just wide and long enough for a man to lie down on it. In Crete these rock mattresses are sometimes left spread with a rustling blanket of dry thyme. In one I have seen a sort of rough besom of twigs for brushing out the sheep-droppings. Beyond the cave mouth a few round, blackened stones neatly arranged will show where the last shepherd, or thousand shepherds one after the other, lit a fire. Such pastoral resting-places are hotching with sheep-ticks and fleas; but they are redolent too of the beginnings of our race and faith.

AYII TRIPITI

The Paterakis family are as it were the chieftains of their district in the White Mountains of Crete, and of Koustoyerako, a village of some 40 souls all more or less related and all acknowledging a kind of clan authority.

The first of the Paterakis brothers whom we encountered was a magnificent, black-avised brigand who had won the King's Medal for bravery in the last war. Later in his house he shyly showed it to us, explaining that he did so only because it was "something English". His brother Manoli, for whom we had brought a letter, was up the mountain with his flock, on the splendid, sun-drenched morning when we reached the village. But the third brother, Vardhis — the accepted brigand of brigands albeit he was still lame from a war-wound — made us welcome with wine and *tsikoudhia**, tomatoes, cheese dipped in honey, and stirring tales of the war and the German occupation.

Presently a short walk was suggested and we were led up to the rock above the village to see a little, squat, arched and white-washed church with a huge bronze bell slung from a gallows beside it. The church was reputed to be seventeenth-century. The inside was cindery with crumbled and partly-effaced frescoes, but one, still comparatively undamaged, showed the patron of the church, St George, fastidious-faced, in flaking finery. On the ceiling a gaunt, bewildered Lazarus risen staring-eyed from the Underworld hung upside-down

* A powerful spirit akin to raki. The Cretans hold that it can cure almost all ailments and therefore apply it liberally, outside as well as inside. They disinfect open wounds with it (and it feels like pouring fire on); they rub it on the scalp, against baldness; and into the joints for arthritis.

from his high-sided tomb.

We were taken back to the house, where a gigantic meal had been prepared for us. We had only been taken out, we realised, to give the women time to get it ready. We did our best with it, and when we had eaten and drunk to our limits we were led to an upper room, reached by a ladder to an empty door-frame, and there slept away the shreds of the afternoon. Then Manoli arrived and the drink and talk and pledging of one nation to the other began again.

Only a little after dawn the next morning we took to the mountains with Vardhis in the hope of seeing a wild ibex. Not the thinnest shadow of a horn or the scratch of one narrow hoof did we glimpse against the blazing red and grey and white landscape. Not a rock or a tree, however, but had its part in Vardhis' memories of the war. Here twenty men had been killed. Here, on this ledge just below us, he and four men had lain hidden for days, without food or water, while a German search column camped actually on the rock-head fifteen feet above them; where we were now standing. "The cuckolds. You know what was the worst thing? They caught a goat — one of our own, but what could we do about it? — and killed it. Not as you or I would; they were Germans, remember. They tied it up and then one of them kicked its head in with his boot. Like this. Then they strung it up and roasted it, over our very heads; and we lay there chewing our belts from hunger."

When we got back to Koustoyerako in the afternoon another stupendous meal was waiting for us. John produced a flask of whisky; nectar for Manoli, who said he had not tasted the stuff for eight years. He drank it then and there, with chasers of alternate *tsikoudhia* and wine, a staggering feat; then filled the bottle up with *tsikoudhia* and gave it back to us, to take to Xan Fielding on our return to England.

From Koustoyerako we had meant to go eastward through the mountains to Ayia Roumeli at the mouth of the great gorge of Samariá. But Vardhis said that the track — seven or eight hours on foot — had fallen in, leaving at least two gaps too wide for a woman to jump. Instinct was all for putting this to the proof, but the thought of what a bother I should be to the others if it were true prevailed, and instead we set out southward, straight down the mountain to the little harbour of Souyia. Here was a knot of houses by the stony edge of the water, at a place where the huge cliffs opened out to make a widish bay. It had a desolate air, though the houses were lived in and well kept. Someone started to explain that it had once been a prosperous and considerable town. The inn-keeper, another Paterakis, said he would arrange for us to go to Ayia Roumeli by boat — a distance of about fifteen miles by sea, I suppose.

The boat was brought: a cockle-shell rowed by an ancient and noble-looking mountaineer, his legs sheathed in black leather boots and his iron-grey curls clustered close on his skull like those of Olympian Zeus.

We ventured to wonder if, between us, we might be too heavy for his boat. "It's possible" he admitted judicially, "that you *might* have to swim — Can you swim?" Comment was thrust in from all sides. "If you go in that boat, you'll certainly have to." "You'll have to tow him as well; he can't." "You won't have to swim far, though; the boat'll sink before he gets it across the bay." And so on.

We could not let this dignified old man or own resolve be shamed like this: we at once embarked, the three of us, our baggage, the boatman, and his twelve-year-old son; and discovered after a few minutes that if we sat very still and bailed very fast we could make the passage, boat and all. Followed by fading cheers and encouragements from the shore we wobbled away into the evening.

The sun was going down and the cliffs that stretched away before us were red to the foot of the sky. From many hundreds of feet above us they dropped sheer into the sea, and the strangest thing about them was a tide-mark scoring the rocks twenty feet above the water-line. It looked as if it might have been left wet an hour or two before: I have heard that it is between ten and twenty thousand years old, and shows where the island once slept on the water, before some huge volcanic upthrust.

The distance to be done seemed immense in proportion to our size and means of propulsion. Godfrey, a rowing man, offered to do a spell at the oars, but the old man had no mind to be out-done by mere youth and muscle. So he cunningly gave him only one of the home-made oars, the shorter of the two, and made him use it forwards, from the wrong place in the boat; meanwhile exerting all his own strength and skill to maintain his superiority, or at least to confuse the effect. We steered a wavering course along the shadow of the cliffs, through a sea as clear and still as the air; the sunset died in rags of splendour behind us; stars and darkness supervened. The old man, briefly surrendering his oar for the sake of talk, repeated that Souyia had once been a large town. I asked what had brought it to its present state.

"Earthquake damage" he said. "And people drifting away." I could not recall a recent earthquake in this end of the island, but it was not the time to say so.

"There are only two boats left now, besides mine", he went on, "that ply along here from Palaeochora. But in the old days there were plenty. They took cargoes to and from the island out there, too; contraband mostly, I believe, besides passengers and so on. And they weren't little boats like this one, either. Great big things they were, with five and six banks of oars."

Something turned over in my mind. Souyia: Syia, the southern port of Elyras and Tarrha, Apollo's Cretan cities; the birthplace of Homer's forerunner Thaletus. yes, indeed, it had once been a considerable place.

"Palaeochora was a big town too, then", the boatman said dreamily. "And there were others along here. Each one had its own king, and they fought proper wars against each other." He leaned forward confidentially. "You know, it was the wars did them more harm than the earthquake, in the long run." He bent to his oar again and ploughed the wine-dark sea.

Between Souyia and Ayia Roumeli there is only one break in the cliffs where a boat can be brought in safely — even a boat as small as ours. This is Ayii Tripiti; there had been talk before we started of putting in here, to pick up one of the other two post-Homeric boats, which might be there supplying the bee-herds. It had an outboard motor, and could take us the rest of the way. We beached on the tiny strand and halloaed long and loud for Petros; but only *petros* the rock answered, with endless, booming multiplications.

A grey stone shore reached up into a narrow cleft, cliff-flanked on both sides as by a castle keep; the entrance guarded, fifty feet out, by a single, coal-black pinnacle of rock. To one side a tumble of boulders concealed a deep cave, once a store-house for the guerrillas, during the German occupation. The boatman and his son offered us food: loaves and fishes; but we refused, knowing that they had come provided only for themselves. We were all thirsty, and the child insisted that there was water on the beach. Groping through the darkness we found it, a tiny trickle coming out of a rock a few feet above the salt line, caught and led along the horizontal channel of a split and hollowed log. But there was not enough for humans to drink. It was the provision made by the two bee-herds, the only frequenters of the cliffs overhead, for watering their brown flocks when they were at pasture higher up the cleft. The stars were lamp-large overhead. We lay down on the round, grey stones and slept until the melon-coloured dawn.

Ayii Tripiti

AYII TRIPITI

Against the dark transparence of the night
dream-tall and midnight-steep
the rocks stood close and smooth and bulrush-black.
Flakes of the full moon lit the stones below
the margin of the wordless, taintless sea.
And there was water in a wooden pipe,
brought for the bees that day-long, far above,
pastured the thyme. We drank our fill of stars
instead of water, and lay down to sleep.

You were so near us, then, that where we lay
we knew Your shadow on the stainless dark.

MYCENAE

The last deep glory of the dying sun
ran red through Argos, like those lecherous fires
that lighted Agamemnon to death's door.

The dumb stones bore our footsteps, that had once
borne witness to Cassandra's bitter cry
and seen the Atridae sink in fire and shame.

Trembling, we saw the horses far below
thunder and stream across the darkening plain.

Where once the night fell utterly, we stood
and felt the dark blood, and the red despair.

MYCENAE

The Atridae were the descendants of Atreus, king and some say founder of 'Mycenae rich in gold'. Agamemnon, who according to some legends was Atreus' grandson, was chosen as commander-in-chief of all the Greek armies at the Siege of Troy; one of the most unenviable appointments any commander could have. He left Mycenae and its territories, including Argos, Aegina, and perhaps much of Achaia, in the care of his wife Clytemnestra; and to help her, his foster-brother Aegisthus. A classic setting-up for the classical tragedy which duly followed.

Clytemnestra ordered that a chain of beacons be prepared, on crest after crest up from the harbour to the high point of the hills that face Mycenae across the plain of Argos: 'sunny Argos where the horses graze' as Homer called it. As soon as Agamemnon's returning ships were sighted the beacons were to be lit, so that she should have time to prepare a royal welcome for her Lord — or so she said. She met him with gold and kisses, and dealt him death: some say by her own hand, some say by Aegisthus'; and the two of them ruled Mycenae for another eight years, until Orestes, Agamemnon's son, killed them both to avenge his father.

We came to Mycenae once, on foot, at sunset. There were few sightseers then, and we stayed unnoticed until the last of them had piled into the ramshackle 'bus at the gate, and the caretaker had locked up and gone down with them to the little *taverna* still called La Belle Hélène. For we had made up our minds to sleep the night inside the walls. There is no other way of getting quite so strongly the flavour of any place in which history has, as it were, coagulated.

Thus we stood looking outward from the ramparts after the sun had disappeared, as the light was draining away out of the plain; and across it as we watched there came a herd of horses at full gallop, and vanished again into the gloaming. We waited then; and one by one along the heights we saw the last shafts of the day blaze out like the watch-fires of the legend: gold first, then red, then sinking to ash and darkness: as if, for a few moments, the veil of 3,000 years had been twitched aside.

CRETE

Cave-black, moon-blanched,
bound with gigantic silences,
clanging with sudden, feral din
and straight again
lapped in a fierce, high stillness, widening
from crest to granite crest;

time-bleached, blood-proud,
hollow with bull-voiced cavern tongues,
myth-ridden, pierced and crowned with thorns;
and near and far
the hard, strange fingers of the Son of God
touching and proving all.

Crete is a whole subject in itself, but it would hardly seem reasonable to write about the Mediterranean in general, and leave it out.

I have never found, and do not think there can be, any place that gives so strongly the sense of having been holy, for so long, as Delphi. There are older shrines, but God was not in them, or has departed; and it is possession, not tenancy, that leaves a permanent trace. Crete is still enclosed in an atmosphere as strong as Delphi's, but it is not of holiness, rather of significant myth. Christianity is still tentative there, though it is held to with passion. A Cretan in a very tight corner will normally say, as casually as he can manage, "Well, there's always God". But Arthur Reid, of distinguished memory, who fought with the Cretans during the last war, said that once, in the tightest of possible corners, he heard an old man answer "And after God there's Pan".

This atmosphere can be sensed by any traveller from the first glimpse of land onwards. (I do not of course mean those tourists from whom the true Crete is screened by petrol-fumes, hotel carpets, and couriers' patter). It impregnates the gentle-seeming, ominous beauty of Mount Ida on the sky-line; then at closer quarters the great gorges that cleave the mountains; the muttering caves and the mysterious high plateaux. It lives in the people, too, many of whom still have the looks and bearing of the Minoan paintings.

To be in Crete for a week or two is as if there were an intoxicant in the air you breathe. To live there altogether, it seems to me, would be hardly feasible, for the atmosphere makes you feel larger and cleverer and braver and stronger than you really are, and this is bound to lead to trouble.

I could write for a long time about Crete and still not have said a tenth of what matters. But there are others who could do it justice; and one day I hope they will.

A SONG OUT OF THE AEGEAN

Down from the leaning deck, lean down
close to the trails of the spinning foam;
all of your dark red griefs can drown
here in these depths and find their home.

Follow the swallow-fish dipping and slipping the blue wave through
Under the thunder and whiteness and wonder the foam sings true:

Dry your eyes; bow your head.
Here are the tears of ten thousand years,
salter and brighter than you can shed.
White in these clear, bright flakes of light,
makers and lovers of life lie dead
and their bones and arts and their broken hearts
encrust their brittle and sea-ribbed bed.

Down from the leaning deck, lean down;
into the deep stars plunge your hand.
All of your dark red griefs shall drown
here, and be ground to soundless sand . . .

A SONG OUT OF THE AEGEAN

Perhaps it has to do with the clarity of the light, or of the water, or something entirely different; at any rate the Aegean is of all seas the least forgiving and the most consoling. Its quality pervades all Greece and permeates Greek nature, making men see and acknowledge things either exactly as they are or else impossibly glorified, but without the least tinge, the least false colouring, of softness or sentimentality. The people are as harsh as the rocky shores themselves, but with the same hidden springs of vitality, the same volcanic aptness for life. In the soft mists and half-lights of western Europe wrongs can be cherished for centuries, and pity and self-pity twine to each other like honeysuckle and bindweed. But in the clear, remorseless dazzle of the islands inessentials are burned away, and sorrows, enormous in their hour, explode and die like foam bubbles on the indigo-coloured darkness that streams past below the coaming.

Some day I should like to think more about whether man's nature influences his physical surroundings, or at least his estimations of them; or whether it is always and wholly the other way round. Have men's minds so worked, through millennia, that we have now the sensation of a clearer light, and a greater freedom of the spirit, in the Aegean than elsewhere? And will our light-meters (but I do not own one) tell us that Sorrento is every bit as bright as Sounion, while our natures tell us that it is not?

MCT 204

Europa, when the rock-bound lands
against the warm *pounente* pressed,
took the wide horn-tips in her hands
and turned her great eyes to the west.

She rode the sunset down and saw
the isles like ingots melt and run.
We, far above the mountain floor,
through cloudy dawn-fields hunt the sun,

and see the summits and defiles,
the cragged and cruel spines that seem
to lurk like slumbrous crocodiles
laid nostril-deep in lakes of cream.

We with our borrowed eagles' view,
she as she labours in the foam,
across the barren crests pursue
the uncharted country that is home.

Dull and often uncomfortable as air travel has become, I still cannot pass an airfield without a certain lift of the heart. This is the gateway to . . . to what? To new worlds, perhaps, or to loved and familiar ones. But that is not really the point. It is the journey itself that raises the temperature of the mind.

To fly over Greece and the islands is to look down at the history of our race. But it is not just that glimpse down the tunnel of time that sets ideas alight: it is the sense of imminent discovery, in more terms than those of latitude and longitude. Man's primal longing for flight perhaps has less to do with finding new lands than with re-finding the oldest of all. The legend of Icarus, it may be, reflects our sense of exile more than the outward thrust of desire to explore.

The Pounente is a westerly wind, named from the Latin *ponere* 'to place' – where the sun is set down. Besides their classical names the Mediterranean winds have names in the *lingua franca*, that mixture of Latin and Romance tongues and Arabic which trading and crusading made current, before Constantinople fell and life turned serious. Gregale is still the Greek wind, blowing down the Aegean, Levante the easterly; and many others besides the more widely-known Sirocco and Khamsin. They have been the bearers of ships and ideas and civilisations, sowing the seeds of thought like thistledown on any shore they touched. 'Say me, where was God when he made Heaven and Earth?' a mediaeval monk asked; and answered himself 'I say, in the further end of the wind.'

FOR AMPHIARAOS

Deathless, the terror of that end:
the sea upflung, the frantic hooves
and groaning earth, trees tossed aside
like straws; flared, panic nostrils: fall
of rock on grinding rock poured down
and darkness over all.

⋆ ⋆ ⋆

So in this hollow, grassy cleft
of silence and of living sun
you have your sacred, wooded place.
The rocks that hold your brimming spring
are rough and warm, like hands that guard
a loved and living thing.

In March the grass and brambled walls
are foam-capped with anemones.
Spiders make cradles in the thyme
and tortoises at pasture there
scuffing their feet in marble-dust
at leisure crop and stare.
Revenge is dead, and Thebes a dream,
and grass and sun and peace supreme.

AMPHIARAOS

Amphiaraos was the Wise Man in the fratricidal war of the Seven against Thebes. He saw that the proposed campaign must bring disaster, and tried to persuade the others against it; but in the end surrendered his judgment to a woman, who chose war, for the sake of a tale about a necklace. The destruction by the Gods, that Amphiaraos had warned the others of, duly fell on them; and although he himself survived the battle, the earth opened as he drove homewards along the shore, and swallowed chariot, horses, and all.

The Amphiareion to-day is an archaeological site lying in a little, steep-sided, seaward-facing gorge, as if the mountain there could well have opened its rock jaws once. It holds the remains of a small amphitheatre, a long stoa, and enough statuary, inscriptions, and votive tiles to make clear that it was once not just a shrine where dream-therapy was practised, but one where cures were effected on a scale to attract comparison with Lourdes. And it still has an atmosphere of tranquillity and peace hard to describe, and marvellous to breathe. This puzzled me at first, for in my ignorance I had supposed the story of Amphiaraos' destruction to imply the same divine vengeance on him as the rest of the Seven incurred. It was not for some years that I learned my mistake. There is another version of the legend, which holds that Zeus as it were carried off Amphiaraos, for the sake of his wisdom, instead of letting him taste death; and thereafter he was not a God turned mortal but a mortal turned God. The message left behind is, I think, that death is no subject for fear.

When I first went to the Amphiareion there was no road to it. We walked for two and a half hours through

78

the pine woods, taking a rough bearing when we could get a glimpse of them on the mountains of Euboea, still snow-topped, across the strait, and the whole floor of the little gully awash with wild flowers. But even today, with a wire fence round the site and a custodian in a hut at the gate, it has few visitors, and its tranquillity is intact.

CA' LEONI

One on another the shadow-stains trickle
over the green–black, liquid stones,
crowned and carved, in the strident sunlight
crumbling to maculous undertones.

Let down the cord from the garlanded window
and drink black night from the well of the day.
Splendour and squalor shall gleam together,
liquescent, putrescent, black-gilt with decay.

Kissing the sea-crust, the pigeon-clad silence
bears up a bell-weight of sea-bronze sound.
Shivers the blade to the nacreous water
lapping the slips where the life lies drowned.

I was lucky in the way in which I first saw Venice.

Chance had brought me up the Adriatic on a creaky, leaky little Greek passenger steamer, and I found myself standing on the Riva dei Schiavoni, the Slaves' Quay, enraptured, almost penniless, but slave to no man.

There was a good *pensione* there. I could not pay the *padrona's* price so asked if she could recommend me a room in a decent house. She took me to her sister's: to a cellar of great beauty, with massive arches.

Next day I called on an American whom I had met in Greece a year earlier, and who had asked me to visit her in Venice. I expected that she would have no idea we had ever met. But I did her less than justice, and she offered me kindness and hospitality without stint. Her great palazzo, built in the seventeenth century and still unfinished, was entered from the back by a little water-gate and a flight of worn stone steps into the narrowest of runnels, the Ca' Leoni: a gondola can just glide along it. The great stone doorway was guarded by two shi-tzu dogs — then almost unknown in Europe.

Inside, the palazzo was filled with her own choice out of a famous collection of modern art. The sheer quantity overwhelmed; but even I, who have never understood what the art of this century seeks to communicate, nor even the language that it speaks in, could not but realise that there were things here of rare quality. And the cellars, where the main living rooms were, removed one at the first step into a world of fable and fairytale, for their great stretches of white-washed stone wall were covered with free-hand charcoal drawings by Jean Cocteau, beautiful, violent, free-flowing, and as near to real life as the tale of Beauty and the Beast.

But Venice itself was stronger than any of these rivals to satiate the eyes and mind. The lingering taint of greed and treachery seems so strong on it that I think I should shoot myself if I lived there long; and yet the beauty draws out one's heart and soul.

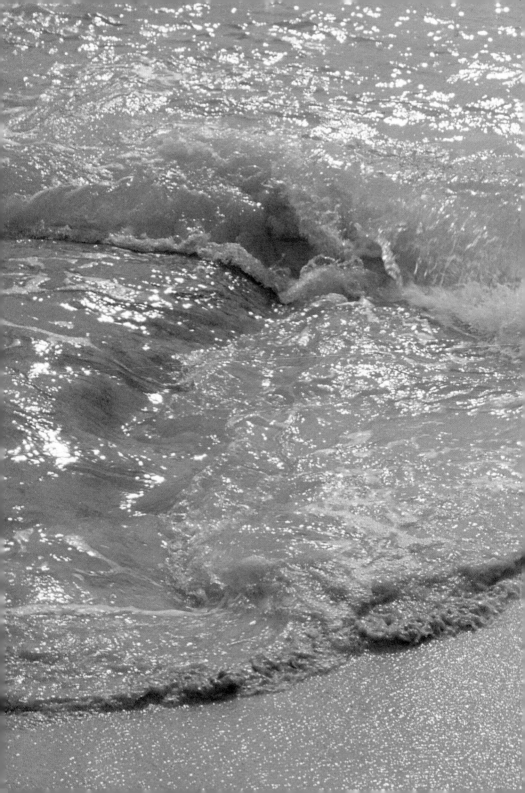

METHONI

This sea is like a net of gold
among whose meshes men discover
that sliver of the truth unsold
that lover can lay bare to lover.

But for the truth that lovers slay
Medusa trails a winding-sheet;
nor all the sea-charm can allay
the stinging lash of that defeat.

The bubbles on the wave-cooled sand
sing once, like swans, before they die
a song the Sirens understand.
Yet they are mute; and so am I.

Below Methoni, lovers lie.

METHONI

Medusae are those great apricot-jam-coloured jellyfish, so like floating sponge-cakes to look at, that drift a foot or so below the surface, combing the water with their long, delicate, fiery fringes.

Tony and I, with our two children, spent a luxurious late summer month, once, not camping exactly but simply living out of doors, between a village in the Mani and the two great sea-fortresses that flank Cape Akritas.

At Methoni a long sweep of white beach, like a curved sword blade, is laid against the land. At its hilt the huge, deserted, silent ruins of the castle — Frankish, Venetian and Turkish — stand with their feet in the sea. Don John of Austria was here in his time, and Villehardouin in his; and Epaminondas and his Spartans were here before any of them. And I rather think, too, that Catherine Cornaro, the last queen of Cyprus, lived for a time here after the loss of her kingdom: a tragic figure and an unconscious bearer of later tragedies.

Coroni, another fortress of the same kind, and with nearly the same history, faces eastwards across the Gulf of Messenia. Beyond the water the Mani stretches, in the mornings like the bluest of smoke-wreaths, utterly insubstantial and remote, though it is scarcely a dozen miles away; and later seeming to hang above the liquid violets and blues and peacock-greens of the sea, in a haze the colours of roses and peach-stones, looking like some vast range — Pamir or Himalaya — seen from immensely far away, its bare granite crests glinting as if with snow. I remember watching, far out, a man rowing a boat, standing upright to lean on his long oar. The movement and general shape were like those of a grasshopper, and I longed to put a giant's finger into the gold-flecked blue of the strait and lift him out like an insect — slender, wire-like legs and transparent wings palpitating, dragged down by the weight of the water on them — and land him on the dark rock mole towards which he was labouring.

At nights we waded to bed round a bluff of black rocks that cut off the beach of the main bay from our own, as it were private, cliff-walled semi-circle of sand and weed. The phosphorus-insects were here; not in flat sheets of brilliance, as in the tropics, but forming a swarm of stars. They were flung against the rocks with each wave, streamed off our advancing shins, and sometimes seemed to dart like fire-flies against the movement of the water.

From the westward-facing shore of the Mani the early morning swims were perhaps the best of all: the water as still as a lake, gold-surfaced with the early sun and glistening with little fishes. Fresh-water springs — about five of them, I think — came up from the sea-bed, making great rings and ripples on the surface of the bay. The nearest was about twenty-five yards out. The water welled up out of the sand, making a kind of wrinkled cloudiness that rose through the clearer sea-water in a spreading column. Within this hung eagerly hundreds of tiny fishes, transparent, green, tiger-striped, brilliant blue and sooty black, noses down, tails and fins quivering with apparent ecstasy. They were beautiful, but somehow disquieting. Were they too, like human spirits, exiles from their natural element, thirsting for the sweet waters of Paradise that they could not name, and drunk with even the least, most adulterated taste of it?

PINDUS

Proteus, before the dawn-wind woke,
up from the sea-bed drove his sheep,
shouldering, jostling, silent, huge:
rough, grey-flanked giants of the deep.

Now, in this incandescent noon
transmuted into living rock,
hardened to granite, oak-tree scarred,
they wait, that sea-forgotten flock

silent, till Proteus call their names —
then shall they shake their shoulders free
and like an earthquake thunder down
to the lost pastures of the sea.

PINDUS

A craggy, shaggy God, Proteus was the herdsman of the deep, and lived among his flocks, from seals to sea-monsters. He was said to be able to take the shape of many other creatures, and to do so, rather than answer importunate questioners. Legend has it that he liked to spend the hot afternoons basking on the rocks of lonely caves or headlands, with his creatures around him: and at such times, if he could be found and caught and held firmly enough, however he transformed himself, he could be made to part with information not to be had from anyone else.

Most of the forms he took were also symbolic of the seasons; and the questions put to him seem to have been in pursuit of practical information, not of prophecies. So he may perhaps have stood for the yearly cycle: for time past and knowledge collected. If so, then it is fascinating, in relation to the facts of evolution, that he be credited with a deep-sea origin and with emergence onto dry land.

I first went to Epirus about 1951, just after the Greek civil war. Only one road crossed the Pindus range and it had been built by the Germans to take the military traffic of their occupation. It was single-lane, with passing-bays, and it had been much attacked by both partisans and weather. There were reaches where the driver must inch in to the cliff-face and slowly and carefully crawl past a broken section; at others he would cross himself quickly and tread hard on the accelerator, and most of the passengers would grip the rail of the seat in front with one hand and cross themselves with the other — from right to left in the Orthodox manner, instead of left to right as Roman Catholics do.

On this journey the 'bus held a few old people with peasant baskets, and about eighteen soldiers going on leave to Ioannina. When the driver called a ten-minute halt at the top of the Metsovo Pass, these all tumbled out; and while some raced off to the one occupied house nearby, in search of wine, the rest put up cigarette packets against tree-trunks and dropped down among the pine-needles to do a little rifle practice. Since this was clearly done in part to impress a foreigner, I accepted a proffered rifle and (luckily having learned what to do with one before, though they could hardly have known that) punctured a packet or two convincingly; and thus confirmed the endearing and enduring Greek belief that, whatever other nationalities may be like, the English are all right.

But it was not until a later view of the Pindus mountains, from the seaward side, that I was caught by their resemblance to a herd of huge, living creatures turned to stone. Then in a moment the myth inverted itself: no longer Proteus hauling himself up from the water to stretch out on some sun-scorched ledge while his flocks browsed the bladder-wrack fathoms below him, but his creatures who had ventured up out of their element and there somehow been doomed to remain, petrified for all time, until he should come to fetch them.

Salamis Bay

SALAMIS

Pink pigs bathing in the bay of Salamís:
and the shine along the shore lights a bright and buried hour:
    The tall ships swinging and the long-lipped scorn;
       the Persian princes sleeping in their power.

Black goats gathered on the shore of Salamís
all the slant eyes wary, the horns that curve and part:
    The small ships stealing through the glass-still dawn;
       the silence, and the hammer of the heart.

Sun full-flooding on the strait of Salamís,
and the water drinks the light, and the dazzle wakes the years:
    The blown pride scattered, and the curled beards shorn;
       the laughter, and the thunder, and the tears.

SALAMIS

There really were pigs there, as I came round the curve of the hill, a dozen or fifteen of them, splashing and squealing in the shallows, backs gleaming and brilliant drops streaming off glistening bristles in the early sunlight. The strait is not more than about half a mile wide — much less in places — and I could clearly see, across on the shore of Salamís Island, the dark, rapid, milling and outward-fanning movements of a herd of goats.

I cannot claim that the pigs on the near shore actually looked as the Persian commanders might have; and yet the sight of them instantly and irrepressibly evoked the battle. For it was here, nearly twenty-five centuries ago, that what may be the most momentous sea fight in European history was won, at the last gasp of what already seemed a lost war. Xerxes had brought the largest army ever assembled (perhaps as many as a million men) down through a Greece already bled white in eight years of war against his father, the great Darius. The Spartan force had just been cut to pieces in the pass above Thermopylae; Athens had been evacuated and the women and children sent to temporary safety. It seemed that nothing stood between the Great King and dominion of all the civilized earth. Decoyed into a move to cut off and destroy the last of the Greek navy, Xerxes sent his fleet into the Salamís strait; and had a throne set up for himself on the hill overlooking it, to watch the ultimate triumph for which he had set out. To bring it about, he had 2,000 great war galleys, and lurking in the coves under the shadow of the island the Greeks had mustered the last of their fighting line: 380 little, battered ships, not much different, I dare say, from many that can be seen in those waters today — and probably not much more orderly and ship-shape. But in their very smallness lay their strength. They could manoeuvre in half the space their enemies needed; and they could keep out of sight for long enough to gain surprise.

Without gunnery, sea fights were an affair of ramming and boarding and hand-to-hand work. The Greeks took on their great opponents not by ramming them broadside-on but slantwise, smashing the oar-blades down the whole side of the vessel in one run. Without steerage-way the towering Persian hulks became helpless; they could not get out of the trap; and morale must have gone too, for their preponderance in numbers of fighting men must have been even greater than of hulls. The loss in vessels sunk was roughly one in ten on both sides; but almost all of the Persian ships left still afloat were taken prize. Watching it all, Xerxes did not yet renounce his dreams of world dominion; but his chance of achieving it had died there. A year later the war was over. Athens had twice been sacked and was to rise again, with its chief glory, the Parthenon, built as a thank-offering for the goddess' help in the Persian War. Had that war gone differently, who is to say but all Europe today might yet be living in a tranced Asiatic twilight?

THE TRAVELLER

Oh but I set my course of air
to seek the lost Hesperides,
    star-gold,
    burning-cold,
ringed round with bitter seas;
and knew that I should find them there,
the hallowed woods, the voiceless bays,
the cool hills where the centaurs graze,
the gold and guarded apple-trees.

Many and fair an island shore
my compass luck has raised for me,
    star-grained,
    summer-stained,
wreathed with the restless sea.
And I have sworn to search no more,
and loosed my limbs along the shade
and let the spirit go, and played
to every air its melody.

Stinging and sweet the sea-wind blows:
another shore is white for me.
    Star-clean,
    silver-green,
soft tides go swinging free
through pearly archipelagoes
and the unfailing season spills
upon the salt and singing hills
its scarlet-flowered anemone.

Light are these alien airs and kind,
the balm to all adversities;
    star-calmed,
    dolphin-charmed:
who would not rest in these?
Yet Ithaca lies still to find,
and brave and brittle as a dream
above the faint horizon gleam
bright wrecks of all my Odysseys.

Time and away I first set sail
and still the foam breaks over me.
    Sun-worn,
    weather-torn,
slight hope my craft may be;
yet she and I, we shall not fail
to find at length, beyond the seas,
the lost, the true Hesperides,
and learn the last reality.

THE TRAVELLER

I suppose that nearly everyone is, at least at times, beset by the sense of exile that I spoke of at the start. It has been with me nearly all my life, and is, more precisely, a sense of having never yet come home. But however intangible, that home is not unattainable. Some day, perhaps only with death, the traveller will reach it. And in the meantime he often catches glimpses of it, and each journey brings him perceptibly closer to it. All real experience brings it nearer; and so, indirectly, the urge to reach it accounts for most of his actions and all of his efforts to learn.

All real travelling (I mean travelling for its own sake, not catching the 6.10 from Victoria) is, I think, a reflection of the other, non-physical journey; and that is a part of what makes it so overpoweringly attractive.

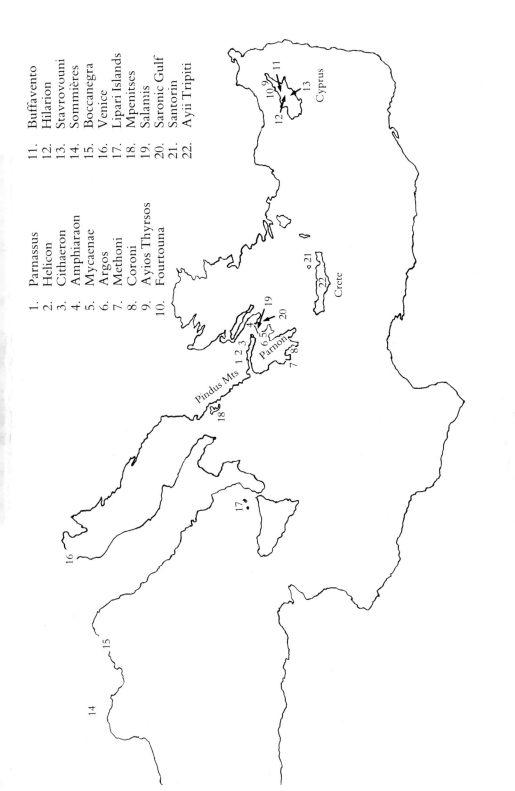

1. Parnassus
2. Helicon
3. Cithaeron
4. Amphiaraon
5. Mycaenae
6. Argos
7. Methoni
8. Coroni
9. Ayios Thyrsos
10. Fourtouna
11. Buffavento
12. Hilarion
13. Stavrovouni
14. Sommières
15. Boccanegra
16. Venice
17. Lipari Islands
18. Mpenitses
19. Salamis
20. Saronic Gulf
21. Santorin
22. Ayii Tripiti

Pindus Mts
Parnon
Crete
Cyprus